THE CABLE STREET
GARDENERS

CHRIS KELLY

Published by: CK editions,
51 Pine Lodge, Tonbridge Road,
Maidstone, Kent ME16 8TA.

Photographs and text
© 2005 Chris Kelly

ISBN 0 9550424 0 2

Print: Aldgate Press

Cable Street Community Gardens
gratefully acknowledges the
continuing support of the London
Borough of Tower Hamlets and
the financial support of the
Neighbourhood Renewal Unit and
St Katharine & Shadwell Trust.

Revenue from the sale of this
book will help to develop part of
the gardens for use by local groups.

Introduction

"You should meet Mr Ali," said Sybil. "He's growing a banana tree in his living room."

I take photographs for the education directorate and the primary care trust in the borough and I'd been working on a project for Tower Hamlets Older People's Partnership. Sybil had helped with contacts and local knowledge.

So I met Mr Ali and admired his banana tree growing floor to ceiling and complete with bananas. He talked about his interest in gardening and invited us to the open day of Cable Street Community Gardens where he has a plot.

At the open day in September 2003 I took the first four photographs. They were of a gardener and poet from Bangladesh; a midwife and former museum curator from the Channel Islands; a London teacher who also writes poetry and a retired transport worker born in Ireland.

It was the start of a year-long fascination. During that time 52 plot holders agreed to be photographed and to talk about how they came to live here and why they garden.

These people, aged from seven to 80, are from a dozen different countries. What they have in common is an appreciation of the natural world and a desire for tranquillity.

They find it in this magical corner of London's East End wedged between the busy Highway leading to Tower Bridge a mile and a half away and the A13 Commercial Road, one of the main routes into the city.

Inside these gates the gardeners cultivate flowers, grow their own food, chat to their neighbours or enjoy some solitude. Trains on the Docklands Light Railway which crosses overhead provide a gentle continual rhythm and a reminder of the world outside.

Haven, oasis, my own little space are words the gardeners use to describe the land here. I'm grateful to them for sharing their precious space and revealing something of themselves.

Chris Kelly 2005

MOHAMAD RAHMAT ALI PATHNI

I have always been a gardener. I started on my father's land in Bangladesh and when I came to live in Birmingham in 1978 I had a garden behind the back yard.

I have lived in Wapping since 1983 and started gardening in Cable Street in 1995. I work here two or three days a week on my own allotment and on other people's plots.

I'm enjoying myself. And it helps my frozen shoulder. I taught my children – two girls and two boys – to garden and my wife often works here too. Many of the gardeners provide food for other people and I regularly give vegetables to friends.

I also write poetry which is printed by local Bengali printers in the Eurobangla News Weekly. And I am a member of a London writers' group. We meet monthly and encourage young people to write.

ANNEMARIE COOPER

I'm a supply teacher and I write poetry. I've had a plot since 1986. I didn't know anything about gardening but I love nature and being close to the earth.

My dad was a very good vegetable gardener. He and my grandfather shared a plot and they were always arguing about it.

I've lived in Tower Hamlets for 20 years. When I started here I thought I wanted to grow flowers then I got into vegetables. I thought herbs, of course, but everyone thinks herbs.

I had some help from B Dahl when I first came and John Grant mended my fence the other day. The older people are good at giving advice.

I love growing sweet peas and big flashy dahlias. Really I like anything that deigns to grow. I enjoy growing tomatoes and digging up potatoes.

JOHN STOKES

I've been gardening at Cable Street since I retired six years ago. I asked one of the nuns in the convent across the road and she said the allotments were for local people. I had no experience but I was brought up on a farm and I found I had an instinct for gardening.

I came over from Ireland 50 years ago. I worked for London Transport for 36 years and missed only nine days. Now I'm at the gardens almost every day in summer and twice a week in winter.

I grow vegetables for myself and my cousin and an aunt. At least half the produce is given away.

ANNA GAUDION

I was born in Guernsey. I've lived in Stepney for the last 10 years and I work as a midwife in Peckham.

I was brought up in the country and I love being outside, hearing birds and growing things so I've always wanted a garden.

I like allotments too, even just seeing them from trains. When I was studying anthropology at the LSE I used to go to Stepping Stones farm and they suggested applying for a plot here.

I've had the plot for three years now. My shed is made from a packing case used to take an object abroad from the British Museum where I was a curator.

I enjoy cultivating flowers so I planted a nature garden. I share my plot with Claire who grows vegetables. Mine is the higgledy-piggledy part and it tends to encroach. My Michaelmas daisies got very big last year.

It's nice having a plot next to Mr Ali; he'll give advice if I need it. I garden all year round and it's lovely to be here.

RAY NEWTON

I have a plot with Agatha. She's been gardening here for a long time. She asked me to help five years ago when her husband became ill. I do the digging and organising and we share the produce. We grow about a dozen different types of vegetables. It's all organic. We don't use pesticides. Agatha is keen on growing flowers too and I want to plant a bank with bluebells.

I retired last year from teaching business studies at Tower Hamlets College. Before that I worked in industry and at one time I was manager of a betting shop. I studied for O and A levels at evening classes and then took a degree course. I became a teacher by chance and taught for 25 years.

I've always grown things. I used to be involved in allotments with my friend Steve Kentfield. It's easier to look after the plot here now I'm retired.

My other interests are local history and football. I'm the secretary of the History of Wapping Trust and a lifelong Millwall supporter.

AGATHA ATHANAZE

I've been gardening here for 12 years. I was born in Dominica and came to Tower Hamlets in 1961. I've done different jobs. I've been a machinist and a cleaner. I live in Wapping now. I have four children, three born in the Caribbean and one here.

I had a garden in Dominica so I did have some experience. The vegetables came first. I grow cabbages; onions; spring onions; runner beans; carrots; tomatoes; rhubarb and kidney beans.

I like flowers too. I've ordered roses from Holland and from Spalding. I just like to come here and grow things. There are two benches but I haven't time to sit down.

ANNIE JOHNS

I was born in London and I came to live in Tower Hamlets in 1996. I've gardened here for five years, at least once a week in spring and summer and every couple of weeks in winter.

The echiums are a favourite. I first saw them at Chelsea physic garden. The plant grows in Madeira and it's not usually hardy but it's doing well here.

I've always grown sprouting broccoli and leeks. And I have calendulas and nigellas among the vegetables. They're nice to pick and take home. I grow broad beans; peas; leeks; chicory; rocket; garlic and shallots. And lots of herbs.

I've always gardened. It's in the genes. My great grandfather was a gardener at Stackpole Court in Pembrokeshire, a great uncle was a gardener and my father grew vegetables. My daughter recently qualified as a landscape architect.

I'm an artist and lecturer. I knew when I was 12 that I wanted to be an artist. I teach adults with mixed abilities.

JEAN CORNE AND ANNIE MCLELLAND

We took over the plot a few years ago. We're sisters living on the same estate by St Katharine's Dock. My husband came to work in the borough in the 70s and we love the area.

We haven't really got going properly on the plot due to family commitments. Emir helped greatly by digging over most of it, he may like to plant something for himself this year.

Annie retired last year so she hopes to spend more time on the garden. We plan to have various flowers and vegetables. Our first job is sifting stones from the soil.

Dad and grandad were great gardeners. We hope to carry on the tradition and enjoy the peace and tranquillity we find here.

JO AND DOUG VICKERS

We've had the plot for about 15 years. We spent a lot of time here when the children were young. They had their own space on the plot so they could dig and grow plants. We put in a pond and the children were able to observe life cycles of frogs, newts and insects.

When I was a child I used to enjoy playing in the garden with my brother and sisters and helping my mother with the gardening so I was keen for our children to have the same experience. We encouraged them to respect living things and not to be afraid of insects. As well as gardening on the allotment the children had great fun playing with their friends.

I grew up in Sunderland and came to live in Tower Hamlets in 1976. Doug was born in Whitechapel but moved away when he was eight and returned to the borough when he was 18.

Since 1989 I've been a support and development worker for Tower Hamlets Playgroups and Under Fives Association. Doug is a pipe fitter. He's working at Wembley stadium at the moment. He enjoys the camaraderie of a large, exciting building project.

ALISON COCHRAN

I moved to Shadwell five years ago because of the allotments and I live just across the road. I noticed them eight or nine years ago when I was living in Bethnal Green. I was born in Salisbury on a hill fort.

I was keen on gardening when I was a child. My sister and I had our own plots in the garden but when I came here I hadn't gardened for years. I knew I wanted lots of flowers but now I also grow salad vegetables and leeks; tomatoes; carrots and radishes.

The soil is wonderful, everything seems to thrive here. John Stokes gave me some advice at first but mostly I've experimented. I've used old Victorian bricks for the paths because I wanted my plot to be in keeping with some nearby housing.

I rescued a stone plaque depicting the Mercer Maiden when a church hall was demolished opposite my home. The mercers exported wool from England and imported silk, velvet and brocade. They supplied the royal wardrobe.

VIRGINIA CATTLE

I was born and bred in the East End and I live in Stepney now.

I've always gardened on and off even though I've lived in flats. I think living in the city makes you appreciate nature.

I haven't done much for the past six months because of my hip replacement but now the weather's fine I'll be spending a lot of time gardening.

I grow potatoes and cabbages and I love my flowers and herbs. I'm worried about bees losing their natural habitats and I try to grow things that will attract bees.

I love it here; it's my bolt-hole.

ANNE HERBERT

I was one of the first gardeners here. I started 15 or 16 years ago. I was born in Wapping and I live in Shadwell now.

Before I had the plot I grew things on the balcony at home. I've learned through trial and error here but I knew I wanted shrubs and vegetables and room for a bench.

I'm growing runner beans, tomatoes and potatoes. At the moment Alice and her children are working on part of the plot.

I enjoy gardening but what I like best here is the serenity.

ALICE AZZOUG

I was born in Birmingham and we emigrated to Canada when I was four. I moved back to this country and came to live in Stepney seven years ago.

I come here with my three children every other day. I'm educating them at home and the gardening is part of their education. We've no garden where we live and we like to do things outdoors.

We're sharing Anne's plot at the moment while we're on the waiting list. I came to know about the allotments here through the Environment Trust.

We've only grown flowers so far but we're having a go at vegetables this year. We're complete novices really. My son Hudhayfa's favourite thing is digging.

MANDA HELAL

I'm from Hertfordshire and I've lived in Tower Hamlets for 26 years now. I've always been keen on gardening. We had a big garden when I was a child and I was given a section of my own when I was very young.

I've had my plot here for three years. My flat in Whitechapel is small and dark so it's wonderful to come here. The wheels are a frame for pumpkins. Pumpkins are creepers and are usually grown horizontally but if you grow them vertically you can fit more into a small space.

I love anything orange with a sweet taste. Squashes and pumpkins are ideal. They are so versatile; you can cook them as a sweet or savoury dish and they keep well.

I grow artichokes and rocket; garlic; kale; cabbage; cauliflower; spinach; asparagus and climbing purple beans which turn green the instant they're cooked.

I've taught pottery in the borough for years. More recently I've become involved in composting and I'm a compost educator for the Women's Environmental Network.

ANDREW PICKIN

I grew up in Finchley and we moved to Shadwell 20 years ago. We spent eight years in Huntingdon when the firm I worked for moved there but most of us came back to London.

I wanted an allotment because I'd always had great fun sharing one with my dad. I had to do what he told me though. I've had the plot for 14 years. We had four children when I started here and I wanted to grow vegetables because money was tight.

The first year's crop was fantastic. It was mainly salad stuff grown from seed. We have 13 children and they all liked coming here until they got to be 10 or 11. The two older ones grow their own vegetables now.

My wife likes coming over to the gardens too. She knows I sometimes come here to get away from the telly or the kids arguing. I'm working here every other day in summer.

ROBIN AND MARIA ALBERT

Robin was in catering before becoming a gardener eight years ago. He was born in Mile End and he's lived in London all his life. I was born in London and brought up in Margate. My family is always trying to persuade us to move out to Kent but we like living in Bethnal Green.

We grow flowers and shrubs in our garden at home but we wanted somewhere separate for vegetables. The fact that everything is organic is part of the appeal. Producing your own pure food is very satisfying.

We grow potatoes; onions; brussels sprouts; cabbage; sweetcorn; strawberries; rhubarb and wild rocket. We have flowers too: poppies; lavenders; roses and a pond that attracts frogs.

Our daughter Grace used to be keen but now she's 13 and interested in other things. I have MS and I can't do so much but I find gardening very therapeutic. I taught dance but I had to give it up 10 years ago. Last year I started learning to play the piano and I love it. It's wonderful to have found another way of being creative.

CONRAD, DONALD AND JAMES KOREK

I garden here with my wife Catherine and our two younger sons, Donald who's 10 and James, six. Our eldest boy isn't interested now.

We've lived in the borough for 14 years and started gardening at Cable Street about a year after we arrived. We have a flat nearby and we like to spend time outdoors. I was born in north London and Catherine was brought up on a farm in Scotland so she has more experience of growing food.

It was hard work preparing the ground but now we grow potatoes; sweetcorn; peppers; courgettes and onions as well as some flowers.

James likes weeding and he supports Arsenal. Donald is a West Ham supporter and he's good at picking up stones and chatting to the other gardeners.

I work for the Home Office in Croydon so I spend a lot of time commuting. Catherine works part-time locally.

Gardening is very therapeutic. It takes your mind off other things.

ANNA GIRVAN AND JOHN GRIEMSMAN

We've had the plot for about 10 years. We're in a 10th floor flat in Limehouse and we wanted somewhere to spend time outside and to grow vegetables.

Our two children were keen when they were young but they've lost interest now. My mother comes along when she's staying with us and gives advice.

I'm from Belfast and I've lived in Limehouse for 25 years. John is from Wisconsin and he's been here for almost 30 years. I work as a librarian in the West End and John is a special needs assistant.

I'm more pleased by the flowers in the end than the vegetables. My favourite is a dahlia that Annemarie gave me. It's a beautiful purple pink and it flowers for such a long time.

GRAHAM KENLIN

I was born in Bermuda. My father was a navy chef and had a land-based job working for an admiral. We came back to England when I was four and I grew up in Hackney. I've lived in Wapping for 38 years and I've had a plot here for about 15 years.

My family have always had allotments. It's very relaxing but I'm a lazy gardener. I've had the odd good year but normally I do just enough to stay credible. I like growing large weeds, anything that's interesting. I try to have 12 plants flowering and that includes foxgloves, marigolds and weeds.

I'm an archaeologist and I work abroad sometimes so the plot gets neglected. I do pottery too; I have a kiln in the spare room. Then there's the motorbikes. I've always driven bikes and I like rebuilding and maintaining them. I don't spend enough time here. You could say my gardening is motivated by guilt.

B DAHL

I grew up in the country so this allotment, which I share with my friend Dick Glasgow, is a life-saver, greenery in the city. We all lost our land when the commons were enclosed. This is a tiny bit of it back.

For me it's sanity. I'm not the only person who's convinced they'd be bonkers but for an allotment. It allows mental drift as you focus on little weeds while the weather changes around you. What you do is natural human activity and you feel a natural human satisfaction.

Eating home-grown vegetables is very nice too. It sidesteps being part of the terrible destruction wreaked on the world and its wildlife by modern agriculture and industry.

BILL WREN

I was born in Wapping and I moved to Shadwell nine years ago. I've had the plot for about 15 years.

We never had a garden when I was young. The nearest I came to gardening was picking hops in Kent. Later I had a woman friend who lived in Burgess Hill, Sussex and I used to grow things in her garden. That's where the greenhouse came from. I put it on the car roof rack and brought it up from Sussex.

I've built a shed here and a pond. There are plenty of frogs and newts. And I've planted up the bank next to the road. It's a wildlife haven now.

I grow potatoes; lettuce; onions; garlic; parsley; broad beans and rhubarb as well as some flowers. And there's a small grassy area with a bench to sit on.

ANWARA BEGUM

I was born in Bangladesh. My father was a businessman and had some land. My seven sisters and I helped mother with the farming. We never had to buy food from the market and we sold bamboo and bananas.

When I was 16 years old I came to live in Tower Hamlets and 10 years ago I started gardening at Cable Street. The four children helped when they were younger but now they are busy with other things. They have to study and help with the housework.

I'm studying too: IT; childcare; maths and English. And I'm taking Bengali GCSE as well as doing voluntary work in a nursery school.

Here I'm growing potatoes; onions; garlic; coriander; tomatoes; rhubarb and different varieties of beans as well as some Bangladeshi vegetables.

There are two reasons for gardening. First, it saves money and second, it's good exercise. I don't want to stay inside and become fat.

JOSEPH MICALLEF

I've had the plot since 1995. I didn't know anything about gardening but my father had a farm in Malta so I knew something about agriculture.

I first came to the borough from Malta in 1955 and settled here permanently in 1961.

The vegetables came first and my wife likes the flowers. But I just enjoy seeing things grow and passing the time here. A lot of the produce is given away. You do tend to get too much at once.

People look at the plot and think I'm an expert but I'm not. I just plant things and they grow.

KHALEDA KHATUN

This is my third year at the plot. It was hard work at first clearing the weeds. I'm growing Asian vegetables and potatoes; spinach; garlic and coriander. And I've just planted climbing marrows.

Growing your own food is part of life in Bangladesh. I came to this country when I was a baby but went back to Bangladesh when I was 11 and lived there for another six years. I had the benefit of learning English when I was young but also knowing my own culture.

Since I came back here I've done many courses including business studies and I've improved my language skills while doing part-time work.

Now I'm an advocate in the NHS. It involves interpreting and promoting health in the Bengali community. And I work two days a week at St Joseph's hospice with people who are terminally ill. I'm always working or studying so I find gardening very therapeutic.

WILL DALY

I was a founder member of the gardens. I was in a nearby pub when Jane came in with another Irish chap and they persuaded me to have a plot. Unfortunately I lost it when I became ill four years ago but John Kelly lets me share his. My son-in-law prepares the ground and I put the seeds in.

I live in Shadwell and I've been in the borough for 27 years. I was born in Ireland and I made a living salmon fishing on a tributary of the Shannon.

I came to this country in 1951 and did building work, mainly in Sussex. One of my brothers came over too but he missed the river and he went home after a while. Then I visited my sister once in Poplar and just stayed. I still go back to Ireland but only for weddings and funerals.

I grow parsnips; lettuce; carrots; cabbage – and potatoes of course. I have health problems so I can't do very much now but I love the peace of it. It's like an oasis.

JOHN KELLY

I was born in Cork City and I wasn't a gardener.
I came to this country in 1943 to work in the
construction industry and started gardening as a
hobby and to help feed the family. I've had the plot
here for more than 17 years. I didn't know much
but I picked it up as I went along.

I've always grown vegetables, never flowers. There's
cabbage; lettuce; tomatoes; parsnips; onions; spring
onions and beetroot. I try to come in every day for an
hour or so but I can't spend too much time here
because I have to look after my wife and I have some
health problems too.

I hate the sight of weeds but I don't throw them out.
I leave them on the ground to let them rot and they
form green manure.

JANE SILL

I was living in Cable Street in the late seventies in a top floor flat with no balcony. One day I went to a community festival and Friends of the Earth had a stall offering plots here. I put my name on the waiting list and kept pestering. I was given a plot in 1980.

I knew straight away how important it was to establish ourselves as an organisation. We had advice from the Environment Trust and Community Land Use and we started making grant applications for fencing and topsoil. We've had a two year waiting list since 1981. At one time I was working in a Job Centre and people used to come in and put their names down for a plot.

I was born in Liverpool and we moved house every few years. My grandfather had an allotment in County Durham and my father was a very good gardener. I helped with weeding and cultivated sunflowers.

I'm growing mainly flowers and herbs now but I'm hoping to have time to plant vegetables again soon.

MARTIN FORD

I was born in Beckenham and moved around a lot before coming to live in the borough near Tower Bridge seven years ago. I feel I've come back to my roots. My grandparents were from Plaistow and they left when the docks industry declined.

I've enjoyed gardening for a long time. For two years I lived and worked in a squatter area in the Philippines. The work included gardening and helping people to supplement their diet. Before that I was a biochemist.

I love working with the soil and seeing things grow and I enjoy the community aspect too. I've had some interesting conversations here. And it's nice having long-term plans for growing vegetables, herbs and flowers.

It would be good to see more wildlife here. I'm considering bird boxes and possibly beehives. I hope to have my own plot in about two years but I'd like to continue to look after the communal part.

STEPHEN AND LAURA BROWN

We live in Stepney and we've just been allocated a plot after being on the waiting list for two and a half years. We've been in the borough since 1997. I'm from Essex and my wife is from Crawley.

We're both keen on gardening but there's a limit to what you can do with a very small terrace garden and window boxes.

We haven't time to be fanatical gardeners but we've inherited some roses and we'll definitely keep those. Laura, who is three, would like to have pink and red flowers. We'll grow simple things like potatoes, tomatoes and blackcurrants and we want a picnic area where the children can play.

I was an accountant for 10 years but I knew there was a possibility of redundancy so I retrained as a plumber. I haven't finished the course yet but I'm already doing plumbing work for friends.

EMIR HASHAM

I'm on the waiting list and I expect it will be a couple of years before I have a plot. Until then I'll be working on the communal area and that part of the project appeals to me too.

My work is computer based graphics and special effects for television and what I like about gardening is the real honest labour and getting my hands dirty. It will be great to grow my own fruit and vegetables eventually.

I've always had a casual interest in gardening. My parents used to garden and I helped as a child. I was born in Sheffield. My mum is a Yorkshire lass and my dad is mainly Asian. I've lived in Tower Hamlets for 12 years now. I haven't a garden at home and there's only so much you can grow on a balcony.

ROBIN, YVONNE AND KATIE GUESS

We live at the other end of Cable Street. There's a small courtyard garden at home but Yvonne and I were used to growing fruit and vegetables before we lived in London.

We love soft fruit: strawberries; raspberries and redcurrants. We had a huge crop last year and we made about 20lb of jam as well as having fresh fruit to eat.

We grow potatoes; onions; dwarf beans; runner beans; cabbage; cauliflower; courgettes; peas and leeks, and Yvonne has planted a mixed flower and herb bed. Our daughter Katie likes planting and picking but not weeding.

Yvonne gardens more than I do but I sometimes pop in on my way home from work. We're both from the south-east. I've been in the East End since 1968 and I worked on the Isle of Dogs as a quality control chemist. Now I'm with the Music Alliance in Oxford Street dealing with composer copyright.

We're in our fourth season now. It's very cost effective apart from the satisfaction of doing something physical and seeing the results.

MONIR UDDIN

I've gardened here for eight or nine years. The plot was completely wild at first. I had to uproot everything and it took about two years to get the soil right.

I used to grow about 60 different plants and vegetables including huge pumpkins. I love experimenting with plants and growing them for their medicinal properties.

I'm a photographer and I also wanted to produce plants to photograph. I've done many different types of work including weddings and portraits. I was involved in the Bollywood film industry, I've photographed celebrities and at one time I had a restaurant.

I've lived in the borough for 20 years. My three children used to come to the gardens when they were younger but they have other interests now.

RAYMOND HUSSEY

This is my second year. It was like Epping Forest when I came here. I live in one of the flats nearby. So far I'm growing vegetables and Ray Newton is going to help me with the planning. I'm learning as I go along.

What I'm most proud of is the brussels. And my runner beans were unbelievable. I had three lots from them. I don't know whether it's the soil or me talking to them.

Weeds are a problem. Sometimes I'd like to use gallons of weedkiller but we're not allowed. So I come in and have a chat. I call them everything bar weeds. My boy comes over to help sometimes but he's not really keen. He likes dancing and night clubbing.

I was born on one of the estates off Brick Lane. I've done lots of things including acting. In my last job I was a dustman but I got trapped by the lorry. Afterwards I could hardly walk.

I still can't do heavy work so the plot's a bit of a mess but it's my little world and I love it. I wave to the people on the train to try and cheer them up.

CHARLOTTE BAGGINS

I've just taken over my plot. There are six tomatoes, six lettuces, a marrow – I'm proud of the marrow – and some night scented white nicotine plants.

I have plans for the best ever bench which I'll build for next summer. There'll be runner beans on three sides so it will be a bench and bean bower. I shall lie in bed thinking about it during winter.

The plot was completely overgrown. I cleared two patches and went to Columbia Road to buy the tomatoes and marrow. I inherited roses and I'll grow some wild flowers. I love old fashioned flowers and I want foxgloves under the bay tree. I'm interested in bee boxes too. I just learned about them this summer.

I've always grown things. Mum was a very keen gardener and I grew up loving plants and nature. We're an allotment family. My daughter had a plot in Edmonton, my niece has one in Leicester and my sister lives on a homestead in Wales. I've been in the borough for 20 years and I live in Wapping.

MICHAEL MULCAHY

I'm one of the founder members and I've been gardening here for more than 20 years. I came to England from Limerick City in 1954. I've been in Tower Hamlets for 42 years and I live in Cable Street.

We had a big garden in Ireland and I love growing things. Fresh vegetables are so good for you too. I know nothing about flowers.

I'm a retired carpenter and I'm at the gardens once a week in winter and every day in summer. Potatoes are one of the main crops. It's worth paying for good seed potatoes. My wife comes down to pick them. I dig and plant and she picks and cooks. I grow lettuce; cabbage; leeks; onions and parnsips as well.

The headstone over there was for my brother-in-law. He was buried in Leytonstone. I hadn't much money at the time so I made the cross myself out of concrete. I took it to the cemetery in my van but they wouldn't let me put it up. I brought it back here and it's been on the plot ever since.

SOMOK ALI

I've had the plot for about four years. We live in a flat nearby and there's no garden.

I came to Tower Hamlets from Bangladesh 30 years ago. The family had a garden there so I knew how to grow things. My wife likes coming here to garden with me.

We grow pumpkins; cabbage; tomatoes and beans, mainly Asian varieties. We always have enough to give away to neighbours.

We have one rose bush which I planted because my wife likes roses. It's good to produce your own food but apart from that it's somewhere nice to come.

SHEILA MCQUAID

I came across the gardens at an open day. It was such an oasis of green and calm that I put my name down on the spot. I've had the plot for a few years now. My children are not as interested as I thought they might be but my daughter comes here sometimes with her homework or with a book and she likes to socialise with the other gardeners.

Gardening is in the family. My parents were horticulturalists and I grew plants as a child but I've only become really interested in the last 10 years.

At first I thought vegetables were more important but we decided on fruit because it's expensive to buy, especially if you want organic, and it doesn't need constant attention.

I was born and brought up in Cornwall and I've lived in Tower Hamlets for 25 years. I'm a housing adviser for Camden council and I work for Stitches in Time on community textile projects.

CARL VELLA

I came to Tower Hamlets from Malta in 1950 and worked for the NHS, mostly as a fitter and stoker in the hospital boilerhouse.

I'm retired and since I took over the plot four years ago I like to come here every day. I grow mostly vegetables: potatoes, cabbages. I'm on my own now so I give a lot of produce away to an elderly neighbour.

Joe helped at first and I had a book once but you really need to try things for yourself.

I live in the flats nearby and there's no garden. Coming here stops me getting fed up. I take my dog for a walk, go to the bookie's and come here. I'd like to bring Pedro more often – he's 13 – but he won't stay in one place.

SISTER ELIZABETH O'CONNOR

Our Order has been part of the local community since 1859 and I came to the convent in 1949. There used to be houses here and the cobbled path in the middle of the gardens was Thirza Street.

The houses were eventually demolished and after a bomb fell nearby the convent bought the land and opened a day nursery for 40 children.

This site was a dumping ground until Friends of the Earth initiated the gardens project. Sister Patricia was one of the first people to have a plot and when I retired from teaching in 1991 I started gardening here. All the sisters appreciate home grown vegetables and having fresh flowers for the chapel.

As a child in Ennis, County Clare, I enjoyed helping my father in our kitchen garden. He taught me to recognise plants and flowers and how to grow them.

Apart from the practical use the gardens are a great place for breaking down barriers. It's especially good that women can feel safe here on their own.

IAN GRANT

I've had the plot for about seven years. I came to an open day and put my name down. I was born in Tower Hamlets just down the road in the old maternity hospital. You can see it from here. We have a garden at our flat in Poplar but mum and dad use that and I wanted a plot of my own.

I had flowers and vegetables from the start: cabbages; peas; beans; asparagus and artichokes as well as cherry and apple trees. Everything grew really well. I was coming here at least three or four times a week until I had my accident. I have a lot of work to do on the plot now.

I like everything about gardening. It's exercise in the open air and fresh food for family and friends.

My other main interest is going to West India Quay once a week. We have an old steam tug built in 1927, the ST Portwey – it's the only working one in Europe – and we have excursions about three times a year to Chatham or Gravesend from Tower Bridge.

MAUREEN FORSTER

I was born in Hampstead but my family were from Jarrow and we went to live in the north-east in 1940. I came back to London in 1964 and moved to Tower Hamlets in 1987. I live in Whitechapel now. My last job was at St Joseph's Hospice in Hackney.

I used to do gardening for the church and Sister Elizabeth told me about the gardens here. I longed for my own garden but I just had a balcony. It's nice though. I've got hanging baskets and even a rocking chair. The geraniums are the most beautiful red you've ever seen.

I've had my plot about four years. It's been mainly trial and error but I did pick up tips from other gardeners. I planted a cherry tree and I've grown potatoes, sweetcorn and broad beans. I'm fond of roses, delphiniums and fuchsias too.

When I come in that gate I feel really at peace with the world. It's my own little space and everyone needs their own little space.

JOHN GRANT

I come from Waterford and I've lived in the borough
for 16 years. I've been in this country for about 40 years.

For me the gardens are about peace of mind,
somewhere to go. I come here for my health's sake. It
relaxes me and puts me in a different frame of mind.

It's nice to see other people here. You can have a
laugh and a joke and pick their brains about the
gardening. But it's not about what you produce, it's
a little haven.

I'm growing potatoes; cabbage; tomatoes; green
beans; beetroot and some flowers. I was always a man
for flowers and there's only space for window boxes
in the flat.

I've had the plot for about seven years and it does me
a world of good coming here.

JOHN DANN AND JENI

John: I started gardening here about five years ago when I gave up work. I was a manager for Ford and I travelled the world.

I used to have an allotment in Romford. I was very serious about my dahlias and I won the vegetable cup there too.

I'm from Brentwood originally and I've lived in Tower Hamlets for 17 years. I have a flat in Wapping now. Apart from gardening my main interests are cricket and travelling.

I love Australia, especially for the weather. I've played golf in Alice Springs in a temperature of 42 degrees. I've been to Australia twice now and we're planning another trip. We do house swops through an agency.

Jeni: I live with John in Wapping and work as a midwife in Kent. I'm from Essex but I've lived in East Sussex for the last 20 years. I've always gardened, mainly vegetables but I love fresh flowers in the house.

KATY, CHRIS, JHONTI AND LUISJON TODD-SIMPSON

Chris was one of the first people involved with the gardens. He helped to clear and establish the site. We've both lived in Stepney for more than 20 years. I'm from Burnley and Chris is from Scunthorpe.

For us gardening has always meant producing good things to eat. We started a deep bed system with troughs for watering. As well as the usual vegetables we explored lots of new types and we kept careful notes about what we produced.

The fact that it's organic is very important. And it's always been a place to escape to, somewhere therapeutic and nurturing. We used to meet here after work, bring a bottle of wine and do some gardening. There's a huge satisfaction in producing good things by physical exertion.

Having children did upset the system. There are different demands on our time now. But we still have the feeling that we're miles away from everything here and it's especially magical in the early evening.

MARY LAURENCIN

I've been gardening here for about 10 years. A cousin had the plot and asked me to help then passed it on to me. I'd never gardened before but I was suffering from depression and sometimes it was the only place I felt comfortable. I learned to garden mainly by watching television.

I'm from St Lucia and I've lived in Tower Hamlets for 40 years. I came to England in 1962 and at one time I did four jobs every day: I worked in a cafe; had a job at Sainsbury's; I was a machinist and I did some cleaning.

There's a patio at home but I always grow vegetables here. I love flowers but you can't eat flowers.